THIS BOOK BELONGS TO:

_____

WELCOME TO MISSISSIPPI

Dedicated to all the explorers.

All rights reserved.
No part of this book may be reproduced in any form or by any means, electronic or mechanical, and no photocopying or recording, unless you have written permission from the author.

ISBN 978-1-958985-33-5

Text copyright © 2024 by Mimi Jones

www.joeysavestheday.com

A Mimi Book

"Mississippi" comes from the Ojibwa word "misi-ziibi," meaning "Great River." The French turned it into "Messipi," which eventually became "Mississippi," reflecting the Mississippi river's importance.

Mississippi was the twentieth state to join the Union. It officially joined on December 10, 1817.

Mississippi is located in the Southeastern region of the United States. Mississippi is bordered by four states: Louisiana, Tennessee, Arkansas, and Alabama. Mississippi also borders the Gulf of Mexico.

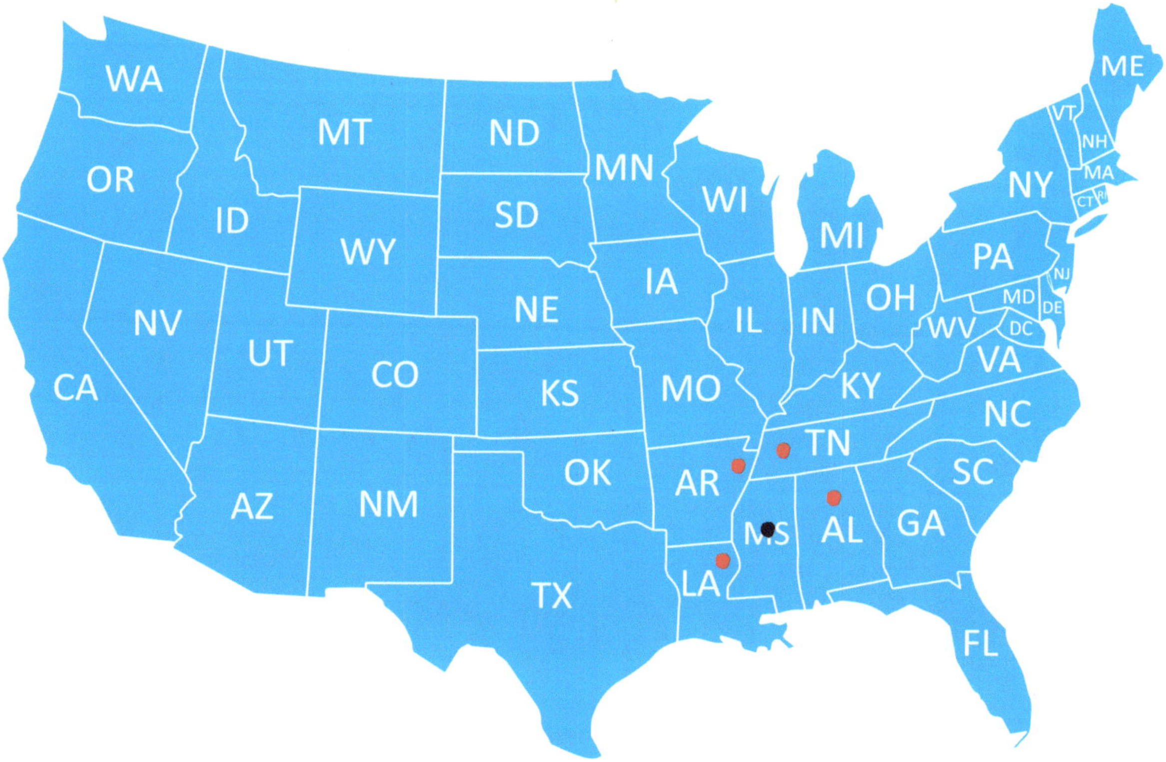

Jackson is the capital of Mississippi.
It officially became the capital in 1894.

Jackson, Mississippi, has an estimated population of about 153,701 people.

Mississippi is the thirty-second largest state in the United States. It is considered to be a medium size state.

Mississippi State Capitol
400 High St
Jackson, MS 39201

There are about 2,940,057 people who reside in the state of Mississippi.

Henry Sampson, who was born in Jackson, Mississippi, gained recognition as an accomplished engineer, author, film historian, and inventor. He is best known for creating the gamma-electric cell.

The USS Cairo Museum in Vicksburg, Mississippi, is part of the Vicksburg National Military Park. It showcases the USS Cairo, a Civil War ironclad gunboat that had sunk in 1862 and was recovered in the 1960s. Visitors can see the restored remains, including the cannons and the engines, and learn about its role in the Union's efforts during the Civil War. The museum provides a hands-on look at Civil War naval history.

Mississippi

There are 82 counties in Mississippi.

Here is a list of twenty of those counties:

Adams	Prentiss	Scott	Lee
Clarke	Tallahatchie	Pike	Jackson
Claiborne	Yazoo	Alcorn	Jones
Lincoln	Winston	Clay	Kemper
Monroe	Sharkey	Lawrence	Montgomery

The Windsor Ruins in Mississippi are the remains of a grand mansion built before the Civil War. The mansion burned down in 1890, leaving behind 23 Corinthian columns. These columns offer a glimpse into the past and are now listed on the National Register of Historic Places.

The Biloxi Lighthouse is a lighthouse in Biloxi Mississippi.
It was built in 1848.

1050 Beach Blvd
Biloxi, MS 39530

The Mississippi River is a major North American waterway, stretching over 2,300 miles from Minnesota to the Gulf of Mexico. It's vital for transportation, commerce, and wildlife. The river has shaped U.S. history and supports diverse ecosystems, making it a symbol of America's heritage and spirit.

Red Bluff in Mississippi, known as the "Little Grand Canyon," features striking red and orange cliffs. Located near Morgantown, it offers stunning views and a challenging hiking trail through forests down to the Pearl River. It's a popular spot for nature lovers and photographers.

The Northern mockingbird was chosen as Mississippi's state bird on February 23, 1944. This bird is known for its beautiful songs and is classified as a songbird.

The official state flower of Mississippi is the Magnolia. It was chosen as the state flower on February 26, 1952, but was adopted on April 1, 1938.

A few nicknames for Mississippi are the Magnolia State, the Bayou State, and the Eagle State.

Magnolia State

Bayou State

Eagle State

The Mississippi state motto is Virtute et Armis. The motto is a Latin phrase that means by virtue and arms or by valor and arms. The Mississippi state motto was adopted in 1894.

The abbreviation for Mississippi is MS.

MS

Mississippi's original flag was established in 1861, while the current state flag was officially adopted in 2020.

Some crops grown in Mississippi are corn, barley, soybeans, sugar beets, and wheat.

Some animals that live in Mississippi are bald eagles, beavers, black bears, groundhogs, raccoons, and white-tailed deer.

Mississippi can get very hot and cold depending on the time of year. The hottest temperature recorded was 115 degrees Fahrenheit in Holly Springs, Mississippi, on July 29, 1930 and the lowest was -19 degrees Fahrenheit in Corinth, Mississippi, on January 30, 1966.

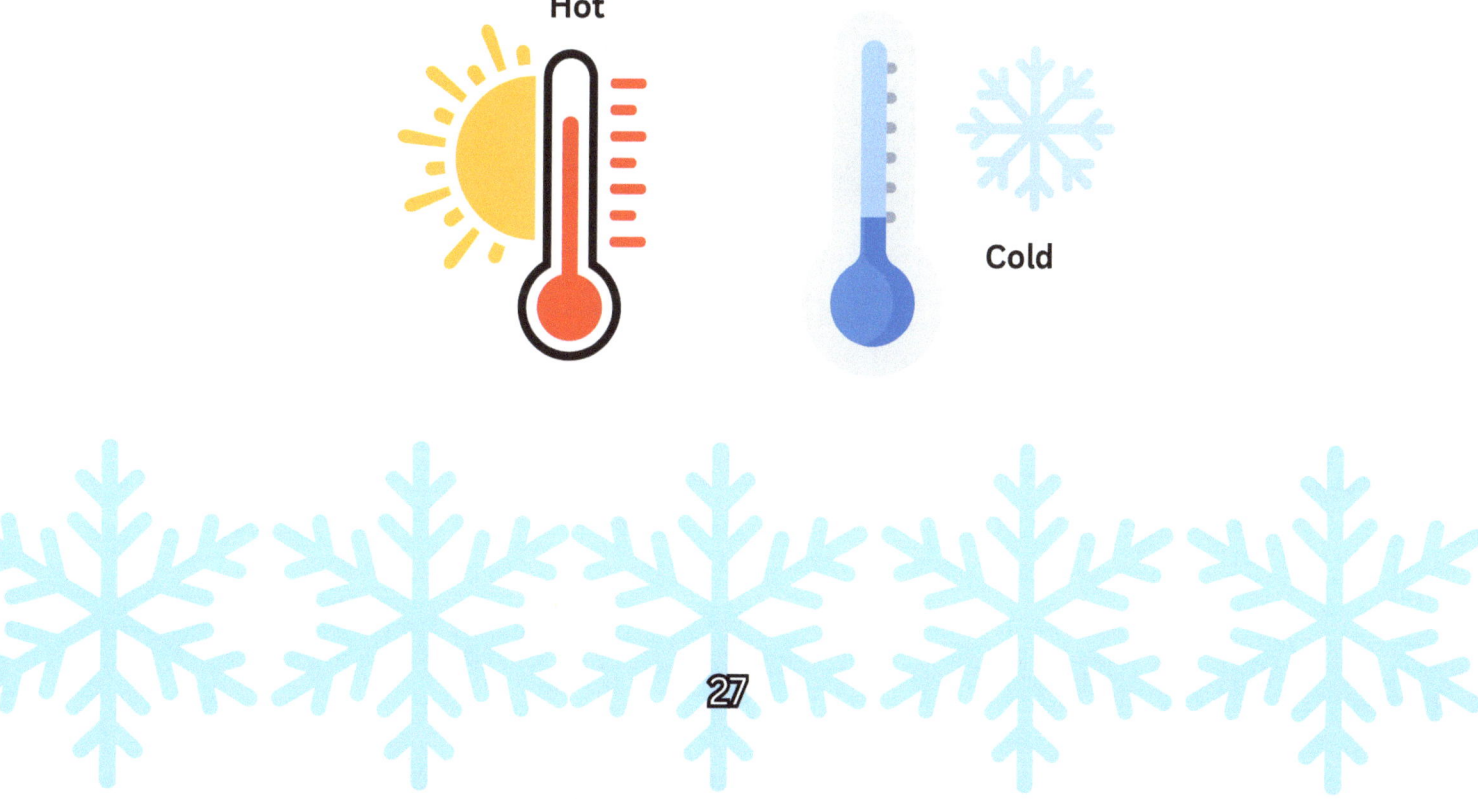

Elvis Presley, born January 8, 1935, in Tupelo, Mississippi, was a famous American singer and actor known as the "King of Rock and Roll." He became popular in the 1950s for blending rockabilly, country, and rhythm and blues. He starred in many films, had numerous hit songs, and won three Grammy Awards. He died on August 16, 1977, but his influence on music and culture lives on.

Gulf Islands National Seashore spans from Florida to Mississippi and features beautiful beaches, clear waters, coastal forests, and historic sites. Visitors can enjoy swimming, birdwatching, hiking, picnicking, and exploring forts and nature trails. It combines natural beauty with history.

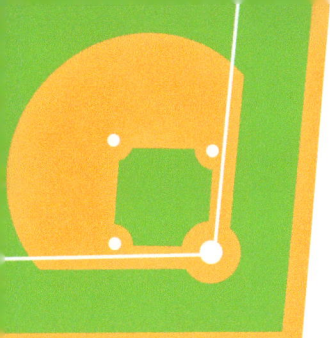

The Biloxi Shuckers, based in Biloxi, Mississippi, are a Minor League Baseball team founded in 2015. They are the Double-A affiliate of the Milwaukee Brewers and play at MGM Park. The Shuckers are known for their distinctive logo featuring an oyster and their dedicated local fan base.

Ole Miss

The Ole Miss Rebels, based in Oxford, are a college football team, founded in 1893. They were originally known as the "Mississippi Flood" before changing their name in 1936. They play at Vaught-Hemingway Stadium.

Cypress Swamp in Mississippi, located along the Natchez Trace Parkway near Canton, has a short 0.4-mile boardwalk trail. Visitors can see water tupelo and bald cypress trees, plus wildlife like frogs, turtles, snakes, and even alligators. It offers a peaceful nature experience.

William Faulkner born on September 25, 1897, in New Albany, Mississippi, is a famous American writer known for his novels and stories set in fictional Yoknapatawpha County. He grew up in Oxford, Mississippi, and his works often explore social, psychological, and racial themes. He won the Nobel Prize in Literature in 1949.

Can you name these?

I hope you enjoyed learning about Mississippi.

To explore fun facts about the other 49 states, visit my website at www.joeysavestheday.com. You'll also find a wide variety of homeschool resources to support joyful learning at home. If you enjoyed this book, I would be grateful if you left a review. Your feedback truly helps. Thank you for your support!

Check out these other interesting books in the
50 States Fact Books Series!

www.mimibooks.com

www.ingramcontent.com/pod-product-compliance
Lightning Source LLC
Chambersburg PA
CBHW040028050426
42453CB00002B/40